The
MILLENNIUM
the unofficial guide!

FATHER TIME

By Bob Fowke
(with cartoons by the same)

Hodder
Children's
Books

a division of Hodder Headline plc

This is *Helen Damnation*, she's a *prophet of doom*. She's bonkers (let's hope), she thinks the world will end when the Millennium arrives! You'll meet many more dismal doom-sayers before you finish this book. Cross your fingers and hope they don't infect you with Millennium Madness too!

CLOUD OF GLOOM

THE END IS NIGH!

Text and illustrations copyright © Bob Fowke 1999

The right of Bob Fowke to be identified as the author of the work has been asserted by him in accordance with the Copyright, Designs and Patents Act 1988.

Produced by Fowke & Co. for Hodder Children's Books

Published by Hodder Children's Books 1999

0340 736127

10 9 8 7 6 5 4 3 2

Hodder Children's Books
a Division of Hodder Headline plc
338 Euston Road
London NW1 3BH

Printed and bound by The Guernsey Press Co. Ltd, Guernsey, Channel Islands
A Catalogue record for this book is available from the British Library

CONTENTS

 Ting-a-ling! Watch out for the *Clock*! Whenever the Clock rings next to a word that means there's a *note* at the bottom of the page. Like here.

WHAT'S IN A MILLENNIUM?

INTRODUCING THE BIG 2000

TIME TO CELEBRATE!

Oh look! There's someone running down the road. They've dressed up as a millipede and they're covered in honey and everybody's spraying fizzy lemonade all over them! Everyone's having fun!

IT'S THE MILLENNIUM, STUPID!

IDEAS FOR CELEBRATING THE MILLENNIUM

A new millennium will begin at midnight on 31 December 1999/1 January 2000. Millions of people will be celebrating. How will *you* go about it?

Give 2,000 zoo animals the day off?

Take out all the light bulbs in your house and replace them with electric egg timers for perfect timing?

Fill your garden with alarm clocks, all set to go off at the exact second of the millennium?

Arrange 2,000 Smarties on your living room floor and eat one every second for the last 2,000 seconds of the old millennium?

Dress up as a millipede and then cover yourself in honey so you can rush up and down your street shouting: 'Honey, I'm Milly the Millennium Millipede and it's the Millennium!' (see previous page)?

GLOP, GLOP

Fill the bath with 2,000 glass-fuls of fizzy lemonade and drink?

The Great Moment arrives!

Let's take a look at how the millennium may really happen:

It's 11.59 pm on 31 December 1999. Hushed silence falls on a mixed group of islanders and rich tourists who have gathered on the eastern tip of Chatham Island, a tiny speck of land in the middle of the vast Pacific Ocean . These people will be among the first to see in the new Millennium . That's why they're staring blankly towards the eastern horizon as if waiting for the Sun to rise - or for the start of a movie.

It's almost time. A large clock has been set up on the beach. The hands grind towards midnight. Nobody moves. The moment they've all been waiting for has almost arrived, you could hold your breath until it does - some people do.

Chatham Island is the nearest inhabited land to the west of the *International Date Line* which is where dawn will first break on the new Millennium - more on that later.

The people on the islands of Kiribati claim that they will be the first - but they moved the Date Line so they don't really count!

Two seconds more - one second - it's there!

Two thousand years have now passed since Year One - whatever that is (well, they haven't actually - more on *that* later). But anyway, the world has entered its third millennium. A New Age has dawned. It's happened.

SUPER QUIZ

A millennium is a thousand years - *mille* is Latin for a 'thousand' and 'ennium' comes from the Latin *annus*, a year. A lot of other words come from *mille* as well. Which of these don't?

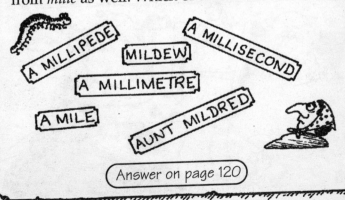

A MILLIPEDE MILDEW A MILLISECOND A MILLIMETRE A MILE AUNT MILDRED

Answer on page 120

So what?!

But *what* has happened? The eastern sky is still dark. The stars still twinkle in the sky.

The onlookers feel a little cheated, even as they reach for their champagne glasses and give a ragged cheer. Everything looks dreadfully normal. If ever there was a time when something big and dramatic should take place, surely that time is now? An entirely new Sun should light up the sky (as the ancient Aztecs believed, see page 118), *Midgardsorm*, the giant serpent which lurks beneath the oceans, should lash the waves into a storm thus starting the end of the World (as the Vikings believed), a ghostly cargo ship should land on some far off shore (see page 101).

Ah well, perhaps far away the *Great Beast* of the Bible (see page 45) is preparing to fight the forces of Good in the battle that will end all battles - the Battle of *Armageddon*?

No.

Nothing has happened. There's absolutely no difference between this minute and the last. If the truth be told, the millennium has arrived with less of an impact than a very small sneeze sneezed by a very small kitten with very small lungs. It's a total non-event. Someone should have told the rich tourists!

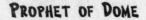

Of course the Millennium will make an impact on the world really, just because so many people are making a fuss about it. Take the *Millennium Dome* for instance:

THE END IS NIGH!

Space inside for two Wembley Stadiums

133,000 SQUARE METRES OF FIBRE GLASS, COVERING THE LARGEST ROOF IN THE WORLD.

SEVENTY KILOMETRES OF STEEL CABLE.

Ten St. Paul's Cathedrals could fit inside it.

Big enough to contain 2 billion litres of milk.

THINK BEFORE YOU BLINK!

A Millennium is a period of *time*, but time is a funny thing: it seems to slow down or speed up depending on how we look at it. Two thousand years may *seem* like a long time to us, but then a day is a lifetime to some types of mayfly which only fly around for a day in total! From the point of view of the Universe, two thousand years is less than a blink of an eyelid. If there is a Mr Universe, he must wonder what all the fuss is about.

MILLENNIUM 2000

BIRTH OF CHRIST

FIRST HUMANS

400 MILLION YEARS AGO - START OF LIFE ON DRY LAND

4,600 MILLION YEARS AGO - THE BIRTH OF THE SUN AND THE EARTH

MR PUNYVERSE

ABOUT 14·5 BILLION YEARS AGO - BIG BANG, THE START OF THE UNIVERSE

At last - prophets of doom!

What's the difference between a *millennium* and a *millenarian*?

I SAID WE'D GET TO PROPHETS.

OF COURSE YOU DID - YOU'RE A PROPHET!

A *millennium*, as you should remember from page 7 if you've got a brain larger than a tadpole, is a thousand years. A *millenarian* is a person who believes that in a thousand or several thousand years from a particular moment in the past something amazing is going to happen to the world, such as for instance: the End of it. There have been a lot of millenarians, most of them mad - and some of them well and truly bonkers. For them a 'Millennium' is much more than just a date. In this book the *Millenniums* of the *millenarians* are written with a capital 'M', and the 'millenniums' which are just a thousand years, or just the year 2000, are written with a small 'm'.

> ## MEANINGS OF MILLENNIUM - PART 1
> *(the only part there is)*
>
> *The year 2000
> *A thousand years
> *A period of a thousand years after which something amazing happens

Millenarians get their name from their belief (still held by many people) that Christ will come again and rule the Earth for a *thousand* years of peace and happiness, and that this would happen several thousand years (or millenniums) after the creation of the Earth by God. Bad people would not be allowed to enjoy the Thousand Year Kingdom of Christ - their doom would be to burn in hell where they belong. That's why *prophets of doom* warn us to change our ways if we don't want to burn in hell.

God's on our side!

People have often found it useful to be prophets of doom. Imagine: you're in a war or perhaps a revolution and you want people to join your side. If you can convince them that your enemy is working for the forces of evil and that the world will come to an end if you lose - well, people are bound to take your side! No wonder millenarian ideas have been used throughout history to help win arguments and wars.

But let's not dwell on the end of the world, let's go back to the beginning. Well, to 'Year 1' anyway.

IT DOESN'T ADD UP!

2,000 YEARS SINCE WHEN?

HOW IT ALL BEGAN – 'YATBOJ' AND THE CLEVEREST MAN IN THE WORLD

The year 2000 means 2,000 years after the birth of Jesus. This system of dating was invented by a monk called *Dionysius Exiguus* (also known as Denis the Little) who lived in Rome sometime around AD 500-525 and was reckoned to be the cleverest man in the world at that time. Under his system, dates *after* the birth of Christ are called AD, which stands for the Latin, *anno Domini*, meaning 'in the Year of Our Lord' - not YATBOJ which stands for the English: 'Years After The Birth Of Jesus' and doesn't exist!

So the millennium will fall on AD 2000, not YATBOJ 2000 - which is a pity because YATBOJ sounds better.

AD and BC are Christian systems of dating but nowadays they are used by many people who are not Christian at all. Recently people have started writing CE, meaning 'Common Era', instead of AD. It can be used in the same way.

Years *before* the birth of Christ are called BC which stands for 'Before Christ', so 2 BC is longer ago than 1 BC and so on.

WHAT A BOJ-UP!

Denis the Little couldn't count properly - his system of dating years from the birth of Jesus Christ doesn't add up. According to Denis, Christ was already a year old when he was born - which was a bit of a bodge-up! Denis' maths problems can't have been helped by the fact that although he spent his life as a monk in Rome, he was born in the wastes of Scythia to the east. Scythian men were wild, horse-back warriors who didn't have much time for education.

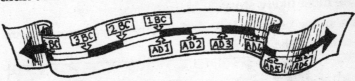

To be truly accurate, the date of Christ's birth should be zero, and AD 1 should be his first birthday. If Denis had got it right, what we think of as the year 2000 would happen in 2001 - we're going to celebrate the millennium a year early!

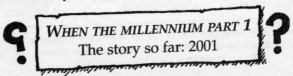

? WHEN THE MILLENNIUM PART 1
The story so far: 2001 ?

SUPER QUIZ

If Denis the Little had to calculate your age, how old would you be now? Remember - your first birthday would be celebrated at the moment of your birth!

Answer on page 120

A WEIGH-IN A MANGER

Christ's age at birth wasn't the only thing Denis got wrong: he also chose the wrong year. And now nobody knows for sure which year it was that Jesus was born in a stable in Bethlehem. Scholars try to weigh the evidence given in the Bible in order to work out when that year was. One thing is certain however - it wasn't year one or zero.

The most likely story

It's a few years before AD 1. The mighty Roman Empire straddles the western world.

ROME

Jesus's real name was *Joshua*. *Jesus* is a Greek translation of Joshua, given to him when parts of the Bible were written in Greek.

At the heart of the Empire, in the great city of Rome, *Gaius Julius Caesar Octavianus Augustus* to give him his full name (63 BC-AD 14), possibly the greatest of all Roman Emperors, sits brooding in his palace. He has won a mighty empire but he doesn't know how many people live in it. How can he know how much to tax them if he doesn't know how many there are?

Servants are summoned to do his bidding. 'Count the people' he orders.

Messengers are sent to the outposts of his empire.

In far-away Palestine the Jewish King Herod (74-4 BC) hastens to do his Emperor's bidding.

Herod was a brute. He married ten wives and had fourteen children, some of whom he killed, as well as murdering a lot of innocent children in the 'Massacre of the Innocents' at Bethlehem.

Shortly after, in a humble stable in the town of Bethlehem in Palestine, a woman called Mary gives birth to the baby who will become known as Jesus.

That's just one of the Bible's versions of when Jesus was born. Unfortunately, the Bible gives us several different versions: it may have been during Augustus' count, or during a Roman 'registration' of people in AD 6, or simply before Herod died in 4 BC. Having weighed the evidence, scholars have decided that the most likely date for Jesus' birth is 7-6 BC.

WHEN THE MILLENNIUM PART 2
2001 (see page 15) - 7 = 1994
We've had it already but nobody noticed!

SWEET MILLENNIUM

Good ideas for the millennium.

All children under the age of twelve to be distributed with a year's free supply of sweets.

A NUMBER OF NUMBERS

Of course neither Jesus nor his mother would have numbered the years taking Year 1 to be the year of his birth. Imagine if we all did that!

Jesus and his mother would probably have said that he was born in 746 AUC or 312, if you'd asked them. 746 AUC is a Roman date and means that Jesus was born 746 years after the foundation of the City of Rome . 312 is a date based on a Greek system common among Jews at that time. There have been almost as many systems of dating as there have been civilizations in the world.

WHEN THE MILLENNIUM PART 3
A minor detail.

The new millennium starts on 1st January 2000 even though the traditional date of Jesus's birthday is 25th December - Christmas Day, but the two dates are near enough as makes no great difference. There's just one problem: Jesus wasn't born in December, or January for that matter, he was probably born on May 20th!

Anyway the millennium has still been and gone.

Actual date of the millennium: 20th May 1994.

 AUC stands for *ab urbe condita*, 'from the founding of the city' in Latin.

SUPER QUIZ

Follow the millennium dog race!

Here are three greyhounds, numbers 7, 9 and 11. They're racing to the millennium, but only one will get there. Pick your favourite then follow the instructions to find out if it reaches 2000 and is the winner.

a) *A good start.*
Multiply the number of your dog by itself.

b) *Flat out!* Add 160.

c) *Still going strong.*
Add another 30

d) *Accelerating!*
Multiply by 10.

e) *Getting tired.*
Take away 290.

f) *Exhausted* (but perhaps triumphant).
Take away another 100.

Answer on page 120

21

OUT FOR THE COUNT!

A NUMBER OF POSSIBILITIES

WHAT'S SO SPECIAL ABOUT 2000?

Why celebrate the year 2000? We could have celebrated any old year: why not 1975 or 2013? They're just numbers after all.

I'M CELEBRATING THE TWOTHOUSAND AND THIRTEENIUM

Thousands are special in our system of counting because we count in tens. This is called the *decimal system* and in our case it means that the numbers up to nine are all written differently but we write the next number as 10 thus going right back to 0, but with a 1 in front of it. So 10, 100, 1,000 all seem to be at the start of a new beginning. Our numbers were first developed in Ancient India and weren't used in Europe before the Middle Ages.

 The earliest examples of modern numbers are written on stone columns built by the great Indian King *Asoka* around 250 BC.

MM!

MM!

No, 'MM' is not what the Emperor Augustus might have said after eating a tasty dish of dormice in honey. At the time of Christ the Romans didn't have the number 0, which was invented by the Indians around AD 800, and the Romans couldn't have written 1,000 or 2,000 even if they'd wanted to . M is the first letter of *mille*, the Latin for a thousand and 'M' is how the Romans wrote 1,000. If they wanted to write 2,000 they wrote 'MM'.

> ## QUIZ FOR REALLY STUPID PEOPLE
> *How would the Romans have written 3,000?*
> (Answer on page 120 - part of Super Quiz)

Until a few hundred years ago most people in the West wrote numbers the Roman way - all numbers were written as letters. For instance 'C' which is the first letter of *centum*, the Latin for a hundred, stands, reasonably enough, for a hundred. It's simple really: the big numbers are written first and you can double

---

This is really why Dionysius Exiguus reckoned the date of the birth of Christ as AD 1 not zero.

23

or triple them by repeating them. But if a small number is written before a big one, you take it away. So this is how they could have written 1994:

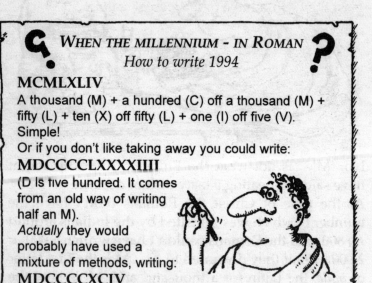

WHEN THE MILLENNIUM - IN ROMAN
How to write 1994

MCMLXLIV
A thousand (M) + a hundred (C) off a thousand (M) + fifty (L) + ten (X) off fifty (L) + one (I) off five (V). Simple!
Or if you don't like taking away you could write:
MDCCCCLXXXXIIII
(D is five hundred. It comes from an old way of writing half an M).
Actually they would probably have used a mixture of methods, writing:
MDCCCCXCIV

MEANINGLESS MILLENNIUMS

At least the Romans used the decimal system - despite appearances their numbers are based on 10. The millennium would be completely meaningless if we used other counting systems. Some African pygmy tribes count *a,oa,ua,oa-oa,oa-oa-a,oa-oa-oa* for 1,2,3,4,5,6, and that's as far as they go (or used to anyway). They would have a problem saying '2,000'.

The native people of Queensland, Australia used to count *one - two - two and one - two and two* as far as four. Anything beyond that they simply said 'much' - but at least they could have had a stab at saying 2,000!

Our decimal system comes from the fact that we have ten fingers and thumbs in total and they're handy for counting with. At least we use both hands; some groups of people only use one hand and have number systems based on five (the *quinary* system). There are several South American tribes who count *one, two, three, four, hand* and German calendars using a system based on five were being printed as recently as two hundred years ago.

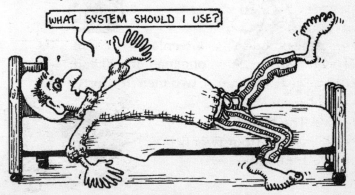

In the quinary system 2,000 is nothing like as dramatic as in our system. Quinary numbers look like this - there are no numbers 5,6,7,8 or 9:

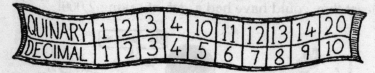

QUINARY	1	2	3	4	10	11	12	13	14	20
DECIMAL	1	2	3	4	5	6	7	8	9	10

Using this system, 2,000 only means 250 in decimal and to mean 2,000 we would have to write 31,000!

TOE BE OR NOT TOE BE

On the other hand, you could say that the decimal system is a bit limited. After all, if we count toes as well as fingers and thumbs we have twenty bits of ourselves to count with. Number systems based on twenty are called *vigesimal*. They were once more common than they are today because more people walked barefoot and could see their toes.

Some Native Americans used it.

AT LAST- THE VIGELLIUM!

Greenlanders count 'one man' for 20 and 'two men' for forty.

The French say '*quatre-vingts*' (four twenties) for eighty.

MILLENNIUM BOUNCE

A good idea for celebrating the millennium

Build a giant bouncy castle, big enough for 2,000 children to bounce in.

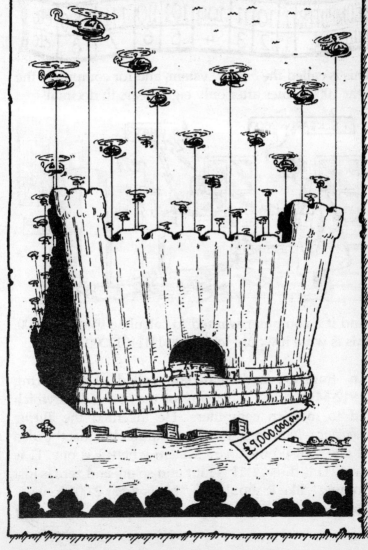

£9,000,000.00

MASSIVE MILLENNIUMS

Even simple systems of counting such as that of the Aborigines are not as basic as the system used by computers. Computers only count with one and zero:

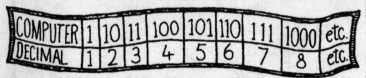

| COMPUTER | 1 | 10 | 11 | 100 | 101 | 110 | 111 | 1000 | etc. |
| DECIMAL | 1 | 2 | 3 | 4 | 5 | 6 | 7 | 8 | etc. |

This is called the *binary* system, and for computers the year 1000 comes after only eight years in decimal!

IT'S NEARLY 2000

SO WHAT?

And if a computer wanted to calculate the year 2000, this is what it would look like: 11111010000.

An English mathematician called Alan Turing (1912-54) worked out many of the basic ideas which led to modern computers. He invented the *Turing Machine* which wasn't a real computer but just the idea of one. It used the *unary* system where 1 is one, 11 is two, 111 is three, 1111 is four and so on, and zero is just nothing - like it should be! This is what 2,000 looks like in unary:

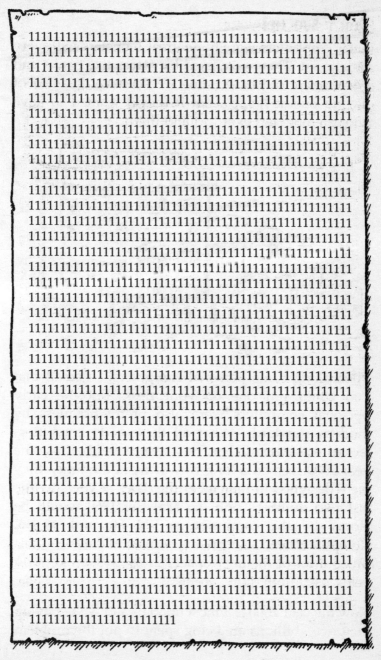

Don't bug me!

Early computers were huge great monsters with very little brain. They were used by places like banks and government offices. No one would have dreamed of having one at home - not if they'd wanted to have enough room left over to stand up in.

I'VE BOUGHT A NEW PC.

Then along came personal computers, so small that you could put one on your desk. But the early personal computers were also pretty brainless by modern standards. What all these early computers lacked was *memory*. For convenience and because the year 2000 seemed a long way away at the time, they were designed to remember the dates of years by the last two numbers only, so May 1st 1960 would be stored by the computer as 5 1 60, and so on. Computers need a surprising number of dates and this saved a lot of memory space, so the system kept on being used until quite recently.

Now the year 2000 is almost upon us and we're paying the price - billions are being spent to put the problem right. There are computers in everything from central heating systems to traffic lights to aeroplanes: if they're not fixed they'll read the year 2000 as 00. No one knows for sure how they'll react: they may pack up and go to sleep, they may have nervous breakdowns - anything could happen. This problem is called the *Millennium Bug*.

When the millennium dawns the best advice is stay well away from trains, planes and anything else where computers are a matter of life and death - just in case.

BILLENNIUMS!

IT'S THE BIG TIME

MMMMM – CHILDREN!

There's a picture of Father Time on the title page of this book. He usually carries a scythe and an hour glass. He started off as the Greek god *Cronus*, one-time lord of the universe who ate his own children - a pretty weird thing to do . But then *time* is a pretty weird thing.

Time is a dimension. For a thing to exist, it has to have the three dimensions: length, breadth and height, and the fourth dimension: time - it has to *last* long enough to be measured. The big difference between time and the other three is that time only goes one way (or so we think). You can climb *down* something you've climbed *up*, you can retrace your steps on a journey - but you can never go back in time.

> Remove any one dimension and a thing ceases to exist. A pure line for instance is only an idea. If it had width so that you could see it, it would no longer be a pure line.

 Weird but not unknown. Female rabbits for instance may eat their young if the young are in danger of being caught by a predator. That way the mother stays strong to have more babies (for more on baby rabbits see page 90).

BANG GOES BEFORE!

Scientists think that Time started when the Universe started, in a huge explosion called the *Big Bang* around 14.5 billion years ago. There's no point in talking about 'before' the Big Bang; there was no 'before' because there was no Time. So Time is 14.5 billion years old. If we dated the years from the birth of Time we would be in the *fourteen-and-a-half millionth* millennium right now, not coming to the end of the second one.

SKULL

HOUR GLASS

SCYTHE

MUDDLED MILLENNIUMS

Our system of dating the years before and after the supposed birth of Christ doesn't do justice to the age of time. Some cultures do have slightly earlier starting points, but these starting dates are still recent compared to the birth of Father Time himself.

The Romans, as we have seen, dated their years from the foundation of the city of Rome in 754 BC. Their year 2000 would have come in AD 1246 our time.

 A *billion* is a thousand million.

The Ancient Greeks mostly dated their years from the first Olympic games in 776 BC. Their year 2000 would have been AD 1224 our time.

Muslims date their years from the flight of the Prophet Muhammad from Mecca to Medina in September AD 662, so their year 2000 will not come until September 2662 our time.

Many Jews date their years from the creation of the world calculated from the Bible as around BC 3762-3758. That means their year 2000 came and went around 1760 BC our time.

Buddhists often date their years from the death of Buddha around 544 BC. That means the Buddhist year 2000 came and went about AD 1456 our time.

Mega-Dates

While Christian, Jewish and other systems of dating look back only a few thousand years, other systems give a better idea of how old Time really is.

Hinduism is the main religion of India. Hindus don't need millenniums, they have *yugas*. By studying the stars, Moon and planets Hindu astronomers long ago decided that the Universe would last for 4,320,000 years in total, which is not as long as scientists now expect the Universe to last, but is still a huge length of time. Hindu scholars divide this huge period into four *yugas* said to be of around 1,080,000 years each.

We are now in the last yuga, the *Kali Yuga*. Kali is the Hindu goddess of Death, usually shown as a four-armed woman who wears human skulls. Sacrifices are made to her at night. The Kali Yuga is reckoned to have started in 3102 BC and there are still more than a million years to go until the end of the yuga - and the end of the world.

For the Ancient Maya people of Central America, all periods of time were gods who carried their time on their backs. By around 500 BC when most Europeans still believed that the Universe was a mere six thousand years old, the Maya were already thinking in terms of millions of years. One of their systems of dating makes even the Hindus look short-sighted - some Ancient Mayan writings probe back *400 million* years.

GRIT YOUR TEETH!

Earth itself is around 4,600 million years old. This is such a long period of time that BC and AD are almost meaningless. Dates are usually given as BP meaning 'Before Present'.

Imagine Earth is a cake. It's so big that there's no point in dividing it into pathetic little slivers called millenniums. What's needed is something we can get our teeth into. Instead of millenniums Earth time is divided into *eras*, *periods* and *epochs*. Epochs are further divided into *ages* and ages into *chrons*. If you want a really long length of time you can bundle several eras together and call it an *eon*.

BP is fine for long periods of time but it causes complications for more recent dates. It's better to stick to BC and AD for that.

SURVIVAL QUIZ

Are you ready for the next thousand years?

1. It's the year 2050. An intergalactic war is brewing. The only safe place away from possible targets is deep in the African rainforest, where the pygmies live - but you have to buy supplies. In the local shop you point at a sack of sugar and ask for three kilos. Do you say:

    a. *Oa-oa* kilos
    b. *Ua-oa* kilos
    c. *Ua* kilos

2. You will be 1001 years old at the millennium, according to your computer's binary system of counting. How old will you be in decimal?

    a. Incredibly old
    b. Dead
    c. 8
    d. 9
    e. 101

3. You wake on the morning of 3500 BP. Which of the following are you most likely to do?

    a. Instruct your robot to bring a bowl of cereal to your sleeping pod.
    b. Pop a piece of toast in the toaster and wait to butter it.
    c. Slice a slab of wild boar with your stone knife and warm it in the embers of last night's fire.

Answers 1-c, 2-d, 3-c

THE FIRST MILLENNIUM

A MILLENNIUM A MINUTE – PART 1

7/6 BC	Christ probably born in Palestine.
AD 1	Christ *not* born in Palestine!
c. AD 30	Christ crucified. Christians start their long wait for his second coming 🕰 .
AD 64	Nasty Roman Emperor Nero blames Christians for the burning of Rome. Millennium expected any day now.
AD 64-313	Everyone nasty to Christians, especially Romans, Greeks and Jews.
AD 90	No Millennium so far.
AD 202	Millennium and return of Christ expected by many.
AD 203	Still no Millennium, sorry.
AD 324	Christianity made a state religion of the Roman Empire by the Emperor Constantine. Christians nasty to everyone else (and to each other).
AD 500	Millennium and return of Christ expected by many.
AD 630s	Muslims conquer most of Palestine and North Africa. Muslims and Christians nasty to each other.
AD 7-900	Sorry, Millennium put off for a bit longer.

Read on to find out more.

🕰 Christ's second coming is called the *Parousia*.

THE ART OF THE START

Let's step back in time, almost to the beginning of the first millennium, soon after Christ had died on the cross, when the world was young (or at least, people thought it was).

Early Christians believed that Christ would return to Earth in a few short years - that the 'Millennium' was just round the corner. By reading the Bible carefully they believed it was possible to work out when the world was created, when Christ would return and how much longer the world would last *after* his return. This is how many of them did it:

The first book of the Bible, *Genesis*, described how God made the world in six days and rested on the seventh day.

The book of *Psalms* in the Bible said: 'a thousand years are but as yesterday' in the eyes of God, therefore (according to early Christians) each 'day' in *Genesis* was actually a thousand years. So the creation of the world would last six thousand years, and was still going on, according to their calculation of when the six 'days' started.

41

The trick was to work out exactly when the seventh 'day'/millennium would start. That was when Christ would return, and when the faithful followers of Christ would rise from their graves and there would be a thousand years of peace and plenty - the Millennium, the *Thousand Year Reign of the Saints* .

The very first Christians believed that this seventh millennium would start in their lifetimes.

PICK OF THE PROPHETS

All early Christians were millenarians although they believed that the Millennium would happen a long time *before* AD 1000. But they weren't the *first* millenarians. For hundreds of years the Jews had been expecting a saviour or *Messiah* to appear and rescue them from their enemies before starting his own reign of peace and plenty. In fact one of the main differences between Christian and Jewish belief is that Christians think that Christ is the Jewish Messiah but that he's come and gone, while Jews are still waiting for their Messiah to arrive.

Belief in the Thousand Year Reign of the Saints before the end of the world is called *Chiliasm* (pronounced 'kiliasm').

Jewish prophets set the pace for all millenarian prophets who came after. A Jewish prophet when he was prophesying could be an awesome sight:

Often they wore ragged cloaks of camel hair with leather belts.

Ezekiel would fall into a deep trance for days on end.

Daniel spoke of 'visions' which threw him to the ground.

John the Baptist lived on locusts and wild honey.

FRENZIED FUTURES
Other religions also had prophets:

Ancient Egyptian prophets always spoke their prophecies in total darkness.

Greek seers speaking with frenzied lips were said to be vessels of the gods' madness.

THE FUTURE FORETOLD

Do you have any prophecies for the future?
Helen Damnation may inspire you:

Lo! I foretell that in the year 2000 the Earth will be invaded by strange creatures from outer space. They will be peaceful and well-behaved and will be called Millennaliens. The Millennaliens will live quietly and honestly, and get jobs as teachers and librarians and that sort of thing.

In the following year there will be major floods and other disasters. Millions of people will be in danger of death, but at the last moment they will be rescued by the Millennaliens who will fly to the rescue in their space ships.

The people of Earth will build a giant memorial in thanks to the Millennaliens, and the Millennaliens will be given lots of money so that they can retire to live in the Carribean.

WHAT A BEAST!

By AD 64, less than forty years after Christ was crucified, Christianity was spreading through the Roman Empire like water through a sponge and there were lots of Christians in Rome. That year a fire burned down most of the city. Emperor Nero accused the Christians of starting the fire and many were burned alive as 'human torches' as a punishment.

NERO WAS ACCUSED OF PLAYING MUSIC WHILE ROME BURNED.

So Nero became public enemy number one as far as Christians were concerned - and especially as far as Christian prophets were concerned. One book, now in the Bible, by a prophet called Saint John the Divine, was very popular. The *Revelation* 🕮 *of Saint John the Divine* told Christians to watch out for *The Beast*, also known as the *Antichrist*. The Beast would have seven heads and ten horns, with bear's feet and a lion's mouth. It would do battle with the returned Christ - and, fortunately, lose. The Beast was probably meant to be Nero, at least in part - millenarians have always been good at being rude to their enemies.

 Another word for 'revelation' is *apocalypse* and 'apocalypse' has also come to mean an ultimate disaster at the End of the World.

45

HAVE YOU SEEN THIS MAN?

The idea of a Beast or Antichrist who would appear just before the start of the Millennium became very popular. In the first two hundred years AD there were plenty of versions to choose from. This is a version described later in the *Testament of the Lord*, the supposed orders of Christ to his followers. It tells Christians how to recognize him:

RIGHT EYE SHOT WITH BLOOD

TWO PUPILS IN LEFT EYE

WHITE EYELASHES

LOWER LIP LARGE

RIGHT THIGH SLENDER

FEET BROAD

BIG TOE BRUISED AND FLAT

Soon there were *two* beasts! Probably around AD 200-300, *Commodian*, a Christian poet, prophesied that Nero would be reborn (by that time Nero had died) but he would be killed by another Antichrist who would appear in the East.

URGLSPFF!

TO THE EAST

Prophecies for the Millennium were coming thick and fast, but then Christians had plenty of enemies to make Beasts of, including the Jews - who were being beastly to them.

MILLENNIUM TASK
Get beastly!

The millennium is drawing close and the Beast could appear among us at any time. Can you draw a really *horrible* beast - worse than the Beast in the Bible? Try to make your beast as vile as possible. Here's an idea to start you off.

The Millennium wasn't just for beasts, everyone got roped in. It was said that the famous Greek emperor Alexander the Great (356-323 BC) had built a great gate to the north of the civilized world to keep out barbarians and that in the final days before the Millennium *Alexander's Gate* would be forced open by the horrible tribes of *Gog* and *Magog*, first prophesied by the Jewish prophet Ezekiel.

CRAZY CHRISTIANS

Christians in Roman times had several beliefs which seem strange today.

In the early days of Christianity, Christians were often

persecuted. They were thrown to the lions in Roman arenas, burned alive or killed in a hundred other horrible ways. Those who died were called martyrs and it was believed that martyrs went straight to heaven, whatever sins they might have committed during their lives - perhaps without even waiting for the second coming of Christ at the Millennium. So while waiting to be martyred, they might as well have a good time. And they did - a lot of sinning took place among martyrs awaiting death in the prisons beneath the Roman circuses! Bishops wrote letters telling them to stop it.

Early Christians had many odd ideas. The *Montanists*, as followers of a prophet called Montanus were called, believed that Christ would appear dressed as a woman. They believed he would start his new kingdom in the wild Phrygian mountains (in modern Turkey). The Montanists honoured women as prophets.

At their meetings the Christians sometimes spoke in strange languages - as Christ's disciples were said to have done when he first reappeared to them after his crucifixion, and as some Christians do today.

If you had gone to church in the AD 250s you might well have found the people divided into several groups. Inside were the good Christians and people who had only done small things wrong. Virgins dressed in white might be sitting at the front, while sinners stood outside. Seriously bad sinners had to grovel on the ground and ask the others to pray for them, desperate for forgiveness so that they could be saved when the Millennium arrived.

The trouble was: it didn't. As early as AD 90 a Christian is recorded complaining that he has grown old and nothing has happened. By the AD 130s another, called Justin, was explaining that God had delayed the end of the world until Christianity could spread everywhere.

SUPER QUIZ

Would you pass as an early Christian?

1. What is Chiliasm?

a. A sickness brought on by eating too many curries

b. Belief in a great disaster at the end of the world

c. Belief in the return of Christ to rule for 1000 years

2. What did Jewish prophets wear?

a. A little pink number with matching accessories

b. Camel-hair cloaks

c. Long black cloaks tied up with a leather belt

3. What did the Emperor Nero accuse Christians of doing?

a. Burning down Rome

b. Holding wild parties

c. Being friends with the Beast from Revelation

4. *How long did God take to make the world?*

a. Six days
b. A thousand years
c. Half an hour

5. *When will Christ return?*

a. In a thousand years' time
b. In your lifetime
c. At the end of the world

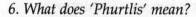

6. *What does 'Phurtlis' mean?*

a. Nothing at all
b. Something holy
c. Something unholy

7. *Who spoke with frenzied lips?*

a. The prophet Ezekiel
b. Greek seers
c. Fat-lips Freddy the futurologist
d. Montanists

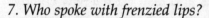

8. *What happens if you hold a party while waiting to be martyred in a Roman circus?*

a. You go to hell
b. You go to heaven
c. The bishop writes you a
   letter wishing you luck

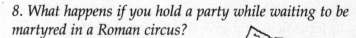

(Answers on page 121)

THE DATE DEBATE (AGAIN)

In those early years the Millennium was always just round the corner. One favourite date was AD 202. When that passed without any ten-headed beasts or second comings of Christ, the Millennium was put back by many to AD 500, all based on calculations from the Bible - but 500 came and went as well.

Then in the 600s things started to look up. Muslims, the followers of the Prophet Muhammad (*c*.570-*c*.632), launched a *Jihad* or 'Holy War' against the Christian lands of the East. Christian armies and towns went down before them like grass before a lawnmower. By AD 638 the Muslims had conquered Jerusalem itself.

At last here was a new enemy! The final days of the old millennium seemed to be at hand after all. Prophecies followed thick and fast. With a new enemy came the idea of a new saviour - the *Last Emperor*. According to prophecies written around AD 660, the Last Emperor would be descended from the father of Alexander the Great (who built the Gates of Alexander - see page 48) and a daughter of the king of Ethiopia in Africa! He would defeat the Muslims, plus Gog and Magog the horrible tribes in the north, then make his way to Jerusalem and give his crown to God.

BEAST COUNT

Who did they think the Beast was? so far ...

IT WAS ONCE BELIEVED THAT EVERYTHING HAD A NUMBER, INCLUDING THE LETTERS OF THE ALPHABET. 666 WAS THE NUMBER OF THE WORD 'BEAST' IN THE GREEK BIBLE — IT HAD SPECIAL, MAGIC POWER.

Emperor Nero
Jews
Muslims
Heretics

 A *heretic* was a Christian whose beliefs differed from the official beliefs of the Christian Church.

THE SECOND MILLENNIUM

(WELL, THE START OF IT)

A MILLENNIUM A MINUTE

1000	Nothing to report. World still there.
1260	Start of the *Third Status* according to the *Joachites*.
1261	No Third Status - sorry.
1304	Start of the *Fourth Age* according to the *Apostolic Brethren*.
1305	No *Fourth Age*. Oh well.
1420	Start of the *New Age* according to the *Taborites*.
1421	No *New Age* after all - perhaps later.
1515	Last date for the *German Millennium* according to the *Revolutionary of the Upper Rhine*.
1516	Whoops! - no *German Millennium*.
1517	Start of the *Reformation*. Pope in trouble, *Angelic Pope* needed desperately.

You'll find all these people in this chapter - and each one's crazier than the one before! (Except the Pope probably!)

THE END IS NIGH - AGAIN

It's AD 999 and the world is approaching its end. People are anxious. They have strange dreams - for instance, a French peasant dreams that bees have entered his body and passed through it stinging and buzzing. On their orders he wakes up, leaves his wife and smashes the cross in his local church - a sign of things to come.

Now it's 11.55 pm on December 31st. Hushed crowds gather in the cities of Europe. Monks chant, priests burn incense in the churches and cathedrals. This is it. The End is nigh - or at least the beginning of the End.

Rubbish! AD 1000 may have been the dawn of a millennium, but few people thought it was the dawn of *the* Millennium. After all, they'd had a thousand years of waiting and they had plenty of other dates to choose from. One new theory was that the sixth Millennium had *already started* when the Emperor Constantine the Great made Christianity an official religion of the Roman Empire in AD 324 (see page 40).

BEAUTIFUL DAMSEL SEEKS HANDSOME KNIGHT FOR DRAGON DUTY

It was the Middle Ages! A time of beautiful damsels in tall head-dresses and handsome knights in armour who protected the ladies against dragons and other evils ...

... in reality, a time of poor peasants tied to the land like donkeys to a cart and often treated like donkeys by the lords and ladies.

Europe in the Middle Ages simmered with discontent. The poor peasants had a rotten life a lot of the time. Heretic peasants in the south of France even believed that this world was *already* hell.

 The *Albigenses*, a heretic group who were finally wiped out in the 14th century.

FOLLOW THE LEADER!

If you were a poor peasant and you wanted to change the way things were, it helped if you believed that your fight was part of the great battle against the forces of evil at the End of the World. Then you weren't just a poor peasant fighting his landlord, you were a soldier of Christ fighting the Antichrist. To make things more complicated, your landlord might well be the local monastery or church. Unhappy medieval peasants found leaders to share their beliefs:

Tanchelm (*d.* AD 1115) lived in the Netherlands and was a clerk in the court of the Duke of Flanders. He visited Rome and saw how the Pope lived in luxury, which shattered his belief in the Roman Catholic Church. He started a new religious movement and took to wearing gilded clothes with gold thread twisted into his hair. He was followed everywhere by three thousand armed followers - and was so well protected that the rich lords couldn't touch him. He married a statue of the Virgin Mary and used to sell his bath water to his followers to be drunk as sacred water. He was finally murdered by a priest.

59

Eon de l'Etoile (active *c.* 1140) also lived like a king. He and his followers terrorized churches and monasteries. He was captured and brought before a council of powerful lords and churchmen at Rheims in France. Eon was probably truly mad. He held up a forked stick and told the council that when the fork pointed up God ruled two thirds of the universe and he ruled the other third, but when the fork pointed down then he had the two thirds and God had the rest - whatever that meant! The council thought he was mad too. Unusually for that time, he wasn't executed.

Fra Dolcino led a movement of preachers who were not priests from 1300-1307. In 1304 Dolcino and his followers made their way to the Alps to await the coming of the *Last Emperor*, who would kill all evil churchmen and start the 'Fourth Age' (another bit of Millennium madness). After defeat at the battle of Monte Rebello, he and his woman friend Margarita were cruelly executed.

The *Apostolic Brethren*, dedicated to poverty and religion, were founded in 1260 by an Italian, Gerard Segarelli, who was executed in 1300.

The Revolutionary of the Upper Rhine (in Germany, his real name is unknown) was active at the very end of the Middle Ages between 1490 and 1508. He claimed that *Germans* were God's chosen people, not Jews, and that the first man in the Bible, Adam, spoke *German* in the Garden of Eden. He also said that Alexander the Great was a *German* (!) and would be restored by a *German* Last Emperor called the *King of the Black Forest* who would murder all priests and start the Millennium of peace and plenty.

The Revolutionary of the Upper Rhine kept putting off the date of his German Millennium, the last date being 1515. His followers were called the *Brethren of the Yellow Cross*.

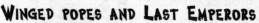

WINGED POPES AND LAST EMPERORS

1. Angels are spiritual creatures with wings who live in heaven. Popes are men who rule the Roman Catholic Church. The *Angelic Pope* is an extra-good pope prophesied for the Millennium - not a pope with wings.

2. Emperors rule empires, but the *Last Emperor* is a specially powerful emperor first prophesied for the Millennium in the AD 600s. The Last Emperor will be on the side of the forces of good at the End of the World.

During the Middle Ages much of Europe, especially what is now Germany, was ruled by the Holy Roman Emperor (usually a German, not a Roman, just to confuse matters), but he and his subjects were also meant to be members of the Roman Catholic Church, led by the Pope. So who was boss - the Pope or the Emperor? Small wonder they often quarrelled.

Millenarians to the rescue! It was time for a new monster: enter the *Antipope*, an agent of the Devil and another invention of the millenarians. If you were on the side of the Emperor then the Pope was *obviously* the Antipope really, and he was fighting against the Emperor for the forces of evil.

But then - if you were on the side of the Pope, your Pope couldn't possibly be the Antipope. Oh no! He was the *Angelic Pope* and the Emperor on the other hand was obviously the *Beast*.

The famous French writer Voltaire said that the Holy Roman Empire was neither holy, nor Roman, nor an empire!

What a joach!

During the Middle Ages there were lots of prophecies to prove that the end of the world was on its way and that the Pope and the Holy Roman Emperor were fighting either for the forces of good or evil, depending on choice.

The *Joachites* (pronounced jo-ak-ites) believed that the world would enter a new perfect age, the *Third Status*, in the year 1260, but that the Antichrist had already been born and would have to be defeated first. Taking the side of the Pope they claimed that Emperor Frederick II (1194-1250) was the Antichrist and was the 'seventh head' of the Beast. They kept on urging people to defeat him right up to the fateful year 1260 when their new age would be born - even though he died in 1250!

Beast count

Who is the Beast? so far ...

Emperor Nero
Jews
Muslims
Heretics
The Holy Roman Emperor, especially Frederick II

 Founder Abbot Joachim (d. 1202). Some Joachites even said that in 1260 the Bible would be replaced by Joachim's writings.

THE HOLY MOUNTAIN

The Roman Catholic church grew very rich during the Middle Ages. It owned huge areas of land and vast monasteries. The common people hated having to pay taxes to support the luxuries of the monks and priests. Frederick II said he wanted to improve things which was partly why the popes were against him.

In the early fifteenth century the *Hussites*, based in what is now the Czech Republic, also tried to reform the church. But some Hussites went too far: they became *Taborites* and Taborites were trouble. Taborites believed that the rest of the world was controlled by the Antichrist and only *they* were on the side of Christ. They left their homes and gathered on hill tops which they called after Mount Tabor, a hill in Palestine. Under their blind general, John Zizka, the Taborites set out to cleanse the world for the *New Age* which many of them claimed would start in 1420. They raided deep into neighbouring countries.

The New Age didn't start in 1420, or in 1421 come to that. But the Taborites kept on raiding until they were defeated by their fellow Hussites in 1434.

NOSTRODAMUS

Michel de Notredame (1503-66) was a French doctor who became a prophet around 1547. He wrote his prophecies in four line verses called *quatrains*. They're so vague that people have been able to read all kinds of meanings into them and Nostradamus is believed to be a real prophet by many. His prophecy for the year 1999 is unusually clear. It says:

The year 1999, the seventh month,
From the sky will come a great king of terror,
Resuscitating the great King of the Mongols,
Before and after Mars to reign happily.

The great King of the Mongols is probably Genghis Kahn (*c*.1202-1227) who built a mighty empire which stretched from China to the eastern fringes of Europe. 'Before and after Mars' could mean anything! Well, maybe Nostradamus was right: maybe Genghis Kahn is coming back, in which case we'd better all watch out.

But maybe he isn't.

REFORMATION!

The end of the Middle Ages was fast approaching and still there had been no Millennium. Many monks and priests continued to live lives of luxury although more and more people complained about it.

In 1517 a German monk called Martin Luther (1483-1546) started what became known as the *Reformation*. He told the Pope exactly what he thought of him. Luther's followers were called *Protestants* because they protested about conditions in the Roman Catholic Church. (The followers of the Pope were called *Catholics* because the Pope is head of the Roman *Catholic* Church.)

Luther translated the Bible into German. All over northern Europe the Bible was translated from church Latin into languages that common people could understand.

Soon everyone who could read could use the Bible to make up his or her own mind about Christianity and about how and when the Millennium and the Second Coming of Christ might happen.

And everyone had a new enemy: *Catholics* hated *Protestants*, and *Protestants* hated *Catholics*. Naturally each side accused their enemies of being followers of the Beast of Revelations and believed that their friends were saints who would enjoy the new Millennium.

By 1530, things were well and truly out of hand. Luther had let the cat out of the bag and he couldn't stuff it back in again. In that year, extreme Millenarian Protestants known as *Anabaptists* took over the German town of Münster. They were sure that the Millennium was about to start. They shared everything, and the men could have several wives - just like in the Bible.

The Middle Ages were well and truly over.

BEAST COUNT

Who is the Beast? So far ...

Emperor Nero
Jews
Muslims
Heretics
The Holy Roman Emperor
The Pope
Martin Luther

SUPER QUIZ

A look back at the last two thousand years.

1. What is a protestant pope?

   a. A pope who complains about protestants
   b. An impossibility
   c. A leader of the protestants

2. Who was the Holy Roman Emperor?

   a. Nero
   b. Gaius Julius Caesar Octavianus Augustus
   c. A German ruler

3. What was Magog?

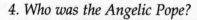

   a. The mother of Gog
   b. A tribe of barbarians
   c. An early Christian prophet

4. Who was the Angelic Pope?

   a. The leader of the angels
   b. An angel called Pope
   c. A specially good pope

5. What did Taborites believe?

   a. That the world was ruled by the Antichrist
   b. That the world was ruled by Christ
   c. That the world was ruled by a blind man called Tabor

Answers on page 122

THE END IS NIGH!

Europe from 1530-1700 was a bear garden where Protestants and Catholics tore each other to pieces like bears in a battle-frenzy. Some countries almost drowned in blood and a whole new country, Holland, came into being.

England was a holiday camp by comparison. Safe on their island, the protestant English were free to experiment.

A MILLENNIUM A MINUTE

1534   Henry VIII and the beginning of the Church of England: no more Pope for the English.

1634   Day of Judgement according to Lady Eleanor Davies.

1635   Day of Judgement postponed. Sinners breathe a sigh of relief.

1642   English Civil War between Charles I and the English parliament.

1649   Millennium according to Fifth Monarchists.

1649   Charles I beheaded by parliament. Republican English Commonwealth begins.

1650   Barebones Parliament, millenarians in charge.

1660   End of English Commonwealth. Charles II returns to England.

1694   Millennium according to John Mason

1695   Mason dead - Millennium put off again.

The madness continues ...

COME YEAR A MINUTE!

1500. England is still Roman Catholic and the English church is still governed by the Pope.

1534. In order to divorce his old Catholic wife, Catharine of Aragon, and marry a new wife, Anne Boleyn, which the Pope refuses to allow, King Henry VIII declares that the Church in England is no longer part of the Pope's Church: it's about to become the Church of England instead.

1534. Protestants become more and more powerful in England. Gradually the Church of England becomes a protestant Church.

1555. Roman Catholic Queen Mary tries to start Catholicism again in England. She burns the protestant Archbishop of Canterbury to death the next year. Mary doesn't last long.

1600 - Extreme Protestants, known as Puritans, get more powerful.

1626. King Charles I collects taxes without the approval of his protestant parliament. Trouble looms.

1642. Civil war between parliament and King Charles I begins. The Millennium is on its way.

Seventeenth century England was awash with sects when the Civil War started, all of them convinced that the Millennium was about to happen.

Anabaptists (remember? we've come across them before in Münster - see page 68) believed that only adults should be baptised 🕰 🕰 .

A BAPTISM

AN' ANOTHER BAPTISM

Their name was used to describe many extreme puritan sects. In Catholic countries, to call someone an Anabaptist was as bad as calling them a terrorist would be today.

Ranters got their name because they used to rant and rave when they were preaching. They believed that the laws of society were meaningless and everyone should decide for themselves what was right and what was wrong (a lot of millenarians thought this).

Levellers refused to accept that rich people were superior to poor people.

Diggers were like Levellers. In 1649 they started a farming community at St George's Hill, Weybridge where the land was shared between them.

🕰 A *sect* is a religious group (usually small) which differs from majority religious opinion.

🕰🕰 *Baptism* involves either sprinkling someone with water or completely dunking them in it. It means that the person baptised is 'cleansed' and has been accepted as a Christian.

Muggletonians believed in their leader, the prophet Lodovic Muggleton (1609-98). They also believed that there were only two types of people in the world: the saved (i.e. Muggletonians) and the rest.

Quakers got their name because they used to 'quake' during church services. They believed that their quaking was a sign of the earthquake at the end of the world prophesied in *Revelation*. More on them later.

Fifth Monarchy Men got their name because they believed that there had already been four other monarchies: Assyrian, Persian, Greek and Roman, and that the Millennium when Christ would rule for a thousand years would be the *Fifth Monarchy*. But then, *after* Christ's rule, the Devil would regain power for a short time. And only after *that* would a favoured few (144,000 to be precise) live in everlasting happiness. Fifth Monarchists expected the Millennium to arrive in 1649.

I'M SO HAPPY.

SO AM I.

THE MILLENNIUM RULES OKAY?

In 1642 civil war broke out between the protestant English parliament and its less protestant king, Charles I. By 1649, Charles I had been bashed into submission. His head was chopped off a year later.

Now extreme millenarian Puritans were in control of England. Oliver Cromwell, the parliamentary leader, opened a period of 'godly rule'. The question was: what was the most godly way to govern the country?

? Harrison, a Fifth Monarchist, advised Cromwell to get rid of parliament and put in its place an assembly of seventy, modelled on the ancient Jewish *Sanhedrin*.

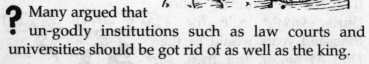

? Many argued that un-godly institutions such as law courts and universities should be got rid of as well as the king.

? It was decided that Jews should be allowed back into England (they had been forced to leave in 1290) where, it was hoped, they could be converted to Christianity, thus fulfilling a prophecy that the Jews would become Christians before the Millennium.

WELCOME

On 4 July 1653 Cromwell opened the new assembly. It is known as the 'Barebones' Parliament after 'Praise-God Barebones' one of its members, also as the 'Parliament of Saints'. This parliament fell under the sway of its millenarian members. They set out to reduce the laws of England to the 'size of a pocket book'.

The Barebones Parliament was a disaster. It lasted less than a year before it was brought under Cromwell's strict control.

ZION ORGANISERS

As previously noted, some people thought that before the Millennium could happen as prophesied, the Jews had to become Christians. Another theory was that before the Millennium the Jews had to return to Palestine or *Zion* - the 'Promised Land' of Israel.

In 1649, a London goldsmith called Thomas Tany decided to speed up the return of the Jews to Palestine. He claimed he was a member of the Jewish tribe of Reuben and said that God had ordered him to lead the

Jews to the Promised Land. He declared himself a Jewish High Priest and set up tents for his followers at Eltham, then in Kent. By 1653 he had still not departed. Growing desperate he then claimed that God had ordered him to kill Members of Parliament and attacked the parliament building with a rusty sword, wounding a doorkeeper before he was disarmed. After several months in prison Tany built a boat and set sail for Holland intending to use that country as the gathering point for his journey to Zion.

Another attempt to journey to Palestine was made by the Ranter, John Robbins. His followers had to train for their journey by living on dry bread, raw vegetables and water. Despite this, so many believers flocked to join him that things got out of hand. Robbins and his wife (who was pregnant and thought she was about to give birth to Christ) were put in prison.

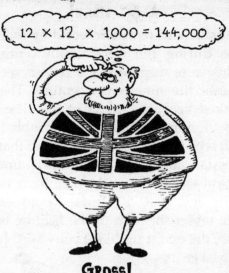

GROSS!

'Dozen' is another word for twelve. A dozen dozens makes 144 and is called a 'gross'. Many millenarians, such as the Fifth Monarchists, believed that only 144,000 people would live happily for ever after the Millennium. The reason for this is that it was prophesied in the Bible that only 12,000 from each of the twelve tribes of Israel would be saved, making 144,000 in all.

You might wonder why on earth would anyone try to save 144,000 Jews if he himself wasn't going to be saved, not being a Jew?

Ah - but what if the British for example were God's chosen people? That would mean that the British were Jews, and then it would be worthwhile saving them! (More on that later.)

A BIT FISHY!

Non-Christians were also infected by millennium madness during the seventeenth century. The *Sabbateans* were members of a Jewish sect which lasted until the nineteenth century. They often went naked because 'Adam in Paradise had no need of clothing'. Their leader, Sabbatai Zevi (1626-77) who lived in Turkey, claimed that he was the Messiah and had been born under the astrological sign of *Pisces*, the fish. To demonstrate the point and that the Jews would return to Palestine under the sign of the fish, he bought a large fish, dressed it up like a baby and showed it off in a basket.

WHO DO YOU THINK YOU ARE?

Seventeenth century millenarians and other sects were always causing trouble for governments. Why obey laws which you think are wrong if it means you won't rule with the saints in a few years time? The Fifth Monarchists (who soon recovered from there being no Millennium in 1649, see page 73) started a rebellion in 1657 which was crushed by Oliver Cromwell.

But Cromwell was a pussy cat compared to the government of Tsar Peter the Great of Russia. After the rebellion of the *Raskolniks* in 1682, each captured rebel was tortured three times and then burned alive if he didn't change his beliefs. The Raskolniks weren't exactly millenarians but 20,000 burned *themselves* alive to 'baffle the Antichrist' as they called Tsar Peter.

THE FURTHER SHORE

The most troublesome of all the sects was the Quakers, also known as the *Society of Friends*. They just wouldn't toe the line.

! Some early Quakers used to run through the streets naked, because Adam and Eve, the first man and woman created by God according to the Bible, went naked. It was not unknown for Quaker men to preach naked and for Quaker women to preach nearly-naked.

! Some Quakers tried to raise the dead from their graves - and claimed success. One girl said that she had been brought back from death by Yorkshire Quaker James Naylor crying 'Dorcas arise!'.

He copied this from the Bible where there is a story that Saint Peter raised a woman called Dorcas from the dead.

Quakers treated everyone as equals and showed no special respect for the rich and powerful. In 1662, Quaker Elizabeth Hooton followed King Charles II around wherever he went, arguing loudly and refusing to kneel to him.

The most fanatical Quakers were totally crazy. James Milner claimed that he was Adam, the first man, and his wife was Eve, the first woman, and that a four-cornered sheet with sheep in it would soon come down from heaven.

John Toldervy believed that flies were the messengers of God and that God wanted all Quakers to stack the sticks, stones, leaves and bricks in their gardens separately.

! Some Quakers wore sackcloth and ashes as a sign that they repented of their sins.

WILD WOMEN PART 1

Millenarian women, and especially Quaker women, were often as wild as the men. They were certainly just as brave.

Lady Eleanor Davis
When Eleanor Davis woke one morning in 1625 at her manor house in Berkshire she thought she heard the voice of the prophet Daniel from the Bible saying: 'Nineteen years and a half to the judgement'.

She wrote to tell the archbishop of Canterbury (the Head of the Church of England) what Daniel had told her, but her husband was fed up with her and burned the Archbishop's reply on the fire. In revenge she prophesied her husband's death and from then until his death three years later she always wore mourning clothes at dinner.

In 1633 Lady Eleanor was arrested for giving out a pamphlet saying that King Charles I was a tyrant. Unbothered, from her prison she demanded that Charles apologise to *her*! After her release there was no stopping her: in 1635 she sat down on the bishop's throne in Lichfield Cathedral and poured a kettle of hot tar and wheat onto the Cathedral wall-hangings saying that it was holy water. She declared that she was the archbishop. After further time in the madhouse and prison she spent the rest of her life prophesying the Millennium and the downfall of the government.

Mary Fisher

Mary was a thirty-year-old servant in Yorkshire when she first became a Quaker. After various adventures caused by her preaching, including prison in York, a whipping in Cambridge and being searched for signs that she was a witch in Boston America, Mary decided to convert the Muslim Sultan of the Turkish Empire to Christianity. This tied in well with prophecies for the Millennium.

Mary set sail in 1657 with three other Quakers. They became separated in Greece and Mary went on to Adrianople alone where she was allowed an interview

---

Her second husband also went mad - hardly surprising! He said he was the son of King James I, hid in his bedclothes and attacked people with his hands and teeth.

with the mighty Sultan. He listened to her arguments and treated her with respect although he did not become a Christian.

Mary lived to a ripe old age and died in America.

ONE MORE TRY!

The main Church of England also had its prophets. Rev. John Mason promised to start the Millennium on Whitsunday 1694. Men and women flocked to his parish of Water Stratford in Buckinghamshire. They shared all their possessions. Weeks passed while believers ran up and down stretching their arms up to catch Jesus as he fell from heaven and clapping their hands. Eighty believers danced round Mason's rectory on 26 April.

Then Mason fell ill and died - having prophesied his own rebirth from the dead. Some followers claimed to have seen his risen body and he had to be dug up just to prove that he was well and truly dead. Despite that, for fifty years people continued to gather on the holy ground near his rectory!

Whitsunday (White Sunday) is the seventh Sunday after Easter.

SUPER QUIZ

Are you mad?

1. Your garden needs some attention. Do you ?..

  a. Stack all the sticks and stones
      neatly in separate piles.
  b. Separate all the sticks and
      stones but leave a big mess.
  c. Do some weeding.
  d. Mow the lawn.

2. Imagine you are married and you think your husband is dying. Do you ?..

  a. Wear mourning clothes at tea
      time, just to cheer him up.
  b. Wear mourning clothes
      at tea time, just to make
      him feel worse.
  c. Get a doctor to give the
      best possible medical advice.

3. You see a four-cornered sheet with sheep in it floating down from the sky. Do you ?..

  a. Praise the Lord and wait for the Millennium.
  b. Go and see a psychologist.
  c. Wonder why there aren't
      any cows or pigs in it too.

Answers on page 122

A MILLENNIUM A MINUTE

From France to England and back to France again ...

1685	Revocation of *Edict of Nantes* by French King Louis XIV.
1689	End of suffering of the *Huguenots* (French Protestants) prophesied for this year.
1690	No end to suffering of the Huguenots.
1702	Huguenots start *Revolt of the Camisards*.
1708	End of the World as per the *French Prophets*.
1709	Sorry - world still going on.
1766	A tenth of London to be destroyed.
1767	London OK - phew!
1792	London and most of the world to be destroyed according to Brothers.
1791	World and London still there.
1792	The Millennium is now! - according to French revolutionaries.
1800/1	Irishman Francis Dobbs says Millennium due.
1802	Dobbs wrong, no Millennium.
2000	(Looking ahead a bit) Millennium due according to Jacques-Joseph Duguet.

Ferocious Frenchmen (and women)

England in the seventeenth century was quite a safe haven for mad millenarians, but France turned into hell on Earth.

France was mainly a Catholic country, and in 1685 the powerful French king Louis XIV revoked (in other words - cancelled) the *Edict of Nantes*, a law which had allowed freedom to French Protestants. After the Edict of Nantes was revoked the *Huguenots*, as French Protestants were called, were ferociously persecuted if they didn't become Catholics.

That same year a plague of grasshoppers swept the south of France: a sign of things to come. Many southern Huguenots believed the prophecies of Huguenot Pierre du Moulin who claimed that the Beast (who he thought was linked with the Catholics) would rule until 2015, but that the persecution of the Huguenots would finish in 1689.

A sort of craziness took possession of the Huguenots as they waited for the end to their suffering. They heard voices in the wind, they followed prophets, many of whom were children or young people, some prophesying in their sleep, others howling like wolves. Their dreams were of victory over the Catholics. One prophet saw an angel flying to France carrying William of Orange (the leader of the protestant Dutch) by the hair followed by 100,000 protestant soldiers.

1689 came and went, but no end to Huguenot suffering. In despair, in 1702 the southern Huguenots rose in revolt . They didn't stand a chance. The iron fist of the French government crushed them within two years. Many were sentenced to be galley slaves. Just a handful of their prophets fled across the water to safety in England.

THE DAY OF VENGEANCE

By the time the French prophets arrived in London, English millenarians had gone a little soft. Quakers for instance were on their way to being the respectable people they are today. The wild French prophets soon found followers among English people who needed a bit more excitement than was on offer in England at the time. Both French and English followers of the Huguenot prophets were called the *French Prophets*.

Meetings of French Prophets were crazy affairs. People might throw each other to the floor while others stamped on them! One prophet is described as grabbing another prophet by the hair and leading him up and down the room.

The *Revolt of the Camisards*.

The End of the World was expected by the French Prophets on 24 March 1708. The weather leading up to the big day was unusual: it rained flies on London - people's clothes were covered in them - and there were violent storms. Many believers stocked their larders with food expecting famine conditions and lived 'the last few weeks' surrounded by supplies of biscuits, beef, pork, and peas. A man called Isaac Owen sold his estate and lived off the profit while he waited for the End.

There was just one problem: Thomas Emes, a leading French Prophet, died suddenly. This troubled the other prophets because they all expected to meet the Millennium together. So they prophesied that Emes would rise from the dead on 25 May and decided that the End of the World had been delayed beyond 24 March (see top of the page).

On 25 May a huge crowd of 20,000 curiosity-seekers gathered round Emes' London grave to watch him rise from the dead. Two regiments of soldiers were needed to keep order. A hush fell on the crowd as a leading prophet called on Emes to rise.

Nothing happened. Emes stayed dead. He didn't even poke a finger through the earth. But undaunted by this little set-back, next morning the prophets explained that of course Emes hadn't come back from the dead - there had been too much of a crowd!

The End of the World was delayed still further.

WILD WOMEN PART 2

Many of the English 'French Prophets' were women.

One stripped off and preached to a horrified audience in a chapel in London.

Another, Elizabeth Gray by name, took off her dressing gown and night clothes in church, then taking a man's wig and hat she sat down 'majestically' in a large chair. She said she was demonstrating a prophecy.

Another burnt a man's face with a flaming handkerchief.

Another seized a man's hat in church and sat on it!

THE RABBIT WOMAN OF GUILDFORD

The 'French Prophets' gradually faded, but their influence lived on. Mary Tofts of Guildford was working in the fields one morning in 1726 when five weeks pregnant. She was startled by a rabbit and in September said she had given birth to sixteen rabbits. The local chemist believed her and in 1752 William Whiston 🕰, a famous mathematician, announced that she had fulfilled a prophecy by the ancient Jewish prophet Ezra.

LOST TRIBES

Meanwhile the idea that the Jews would return to Palestine or that the English were the lost tribe of Israel, or both, lived on. William Whiston claimed that the Jews would return to Palestine in 1766, but before that a tenth of the city of London would fall to the ground and 7,000 important men would die.

1766 came and went but London was undamaged.

William Whiston was successor to the famous scientist Sir Isaac Newton at the University of Cambridge.

The poet Christopher Smart claimed that he was a descendant of King David of the Jews, that the English were 'The Seed of Abraham' (meaning Abraham's descendants, the Jews) - and that Christ would come again to build a new Jerusalem in England's green and pleasant land. Thus making Smart into a prince.

PRINCE SMART

OH BROTHER! (OR RATHER - NEPHEW)

Richard Brothers (1757-1894) was very interested in the Jews. He said he was a 'nephew of God' from the family of Jesus and he started a new religion, the *Anglo-Israelites* . He also announced that in 1791 (later put off to 1795) London and most of the world would be destroyed by an earthquake. Many believed him. There was a massive thunderstorm the day before 4 June 1795, the revised day of doom, and hundreds left London.

EXHAUSTED BY MAKING HIS PROPHECY, BROTHERS LAY ON HIS FACE FOR THREE DAYS AND NIGHTS WITHOUT EATING.

Anglo-Israelites means 'English Jews'.

Brothers' special mission was to lead the Anglo-Israelites to the Promised Land. After a period in the madhouse, this 'Prince of the Hebrews' spent the last thirty years of his life designing the uniforms, flags and palaces of his *New Jerusalem* .

JOANNA SOUTHCOTT

Joanna Southcott (*c.*1750-1814) took up where Brothers left off. The daughter of a Devon farmer, she started prophesying in 1792 and started to gather the 144,000 'hidden Jews' who would rule with Christ after the Millennium. Things went well and she signed up several thousand people. But she then claimed that she was about to give birth to 'Shiloh', a prophet prophesied in the Bible who would take charge of the gathering of the chosen. In October 1813 she prepared to give birth and shut herself in her room. She was sixty-four, far too old to have a baby, but six doctors confirmed that she was pregnant.

Excitement mounted as people waited for the birth of Shiloh, but by November of the following year there was still no birth. Joanna had been laid up for nearly a year. She now prophesied her own death and told the doctors to keep her body warm for four days after her death (just to make sure she was well and truly dead), before cutting her open to find out why Shiloh had not appeared.

 The famous poem *Jerusalem* by William Blake probably refers to Brothers' and Smart's prophesies.

Joanna Southcott died in December. The body was kept warm with hot water bottles and then cut open after the four days were up. There was no sign of Shiloh, although some followers claimed that he had been born already and had gone straight to heaven without anyone noticing!

Sightings of Shiloh continued into the next century.

At last - the Millennium

Meanwhile back in Roman Catholic France - the Millennium had been and gone! The *French Revolution* started in 1789 when the poor and the middle classes rose up and seized control of their country from rich aristocrats and the king. The king and queen and thousands of aristocrats had their heads chopped off by the dreaded guillotine.

The French decided that their revolution was the start of a completely new kind of world. It was so important that the years should be dated from its beginning. In 1792 a new, revolutionary religion was founded and that date became Year One - instead of Year One being AD 1 the supposed date of the birth of Christ. Notre Dame, the main cathedral in Paris, was turned into a 'Temple of Reason' instead of a cathedral. And *everything* went decimal. The twelve-hour day became a ten-hour day, and the seven-day week became a ten-day week - which meant fewer weekends. You can't get much more revolutionary than that!

Unfortunately it was now very difficult for the French to deal with other countries since their new system of dating was so different. The French revolutionary system of dating was quietly dropped in 1806.

CATHOLICS

In the eighteenth century Protestants and revolutionaries had the lion's share of mad millenarians, but there were some Catholic prophets too.

In 1733 the Frenchman Jacques-Joseph Duguet prophesied that the Millennium would arrive in the year 2000 (so we'd better be careful!). But before that happened the Jews would have to be converted to Christianity and return to Palestine.

Catherine Theot believed that the French Revolution was part of God's plan and would prepare the world for the second coming of Christ. Catherine was known as the 'New Eve', after the first woman created by God, according to the Bible.

In 1787, Suzette Labrousse prophesied that events leading to the French Revolution would start in three years, so she was only a year out. She was a tall girl with a squint and she expected to become a 'new being' who would be seen by the entire universe when the Revolution came!

SUPER QUIZ

Are you a believer?

1. *Did Mary Tofts give birth to sixteen rabbits?*
   a. No, only twelve.
   b. Yes.
   c. Don't be ridiculous.

2. *What happened to Shiloh?*
   a. He was never going to be reborn anyway.
   b. He was reborn as a rabbit and lived out the rest of his life on Hampstead Heath.
   c. He went straight up to heaven without anybody noticing.

3. *Why didn't Emes come back from the dead?*
   a. Because too many people were watching.
   b. Because he was dead as a door knob.
   c. Because it wasn't time yet.

Answers on page 123

NOT SO LONG
(SAYS HONG)

NINETEEN CENTURIES DOWN ...

A MILLENNIUM A MINUTE

What comes next? From madness to murder ...

1833   Millennium according to the Russian, Terence Byelozorov.

1836   Millennium according to Lukian Petrov, also a Russian.

1837   Apologies, Russians - Millennium delayed.

1840s   The Messiah has arrived at last! Welcome, James Prince of Weymouth.

1843   Well, perhaps not, James, but this year we'll see the real thing according to William Miller.

1844   Whoops - the real thing is *this* year, not last year says Miller.

1845   Oh dear! - wrong again. Poor William Miller.

1850   Heavenly Kingdom of Great Peace, or *Taiping*, arrives in China.

1870s   North American Ghost Dances may do the trick.

1914   The Millennium begins about now according to Jehovah's Witnesses.

1919   *Vailala Madness* hits Papua New Guinea. All aboard for a brave new world.

1934   Adolf Hitler announces *Thousand Year Reich*.

EURO-LEAK

The nineteenth century dawned on a world which had missed more Millenniums than there are trains in Transylvania. But still prophecies of Millenniums kept on coming. This was the century when Europe ruled the world and European millenarian ideas leaked out from western Europe in large, doom-laden dribbles.

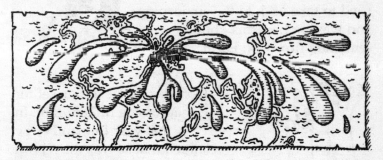

RUSSIAN RAVERS

In 1815 the French Revolution (or what was left of it) was finally crushed at the Battle of Waterloo. That same year, a book by Englishman Young Stilling became wildly popular in Moscow, especially with a sect called the *Molokanye* . The book seemed to say that Christ would start the Millennium at Mount Ararat - a part of the Russian Empire from 1830.

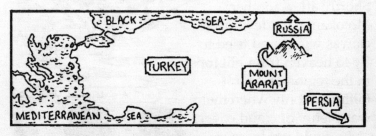

 Molokanye comes from the Russian word for milk, *moloko* - members of the sect drank milk during Lent when it was forbidden.

Terence Byelozorov was a Molokanye. He claimed he was the prophet Elias from the Bible and foretold the exact day in 1833 when he would ascend to heaven and start the Millennium. Crowds flocked to Mount Ararat. On the great day Terence desperately tried to take off into the air, leaping and waving his arms - but he remained firmly on Earth.

IT'S A MIRACLE!

1836 was the next date set for the Russian Millennium. In that year Lukian Petrov claimed that *he* was the reborn Christ. So as to appear extra-convincing, he trained two girls to pretend to be dead and then spring to 'life' at his magic word. He thus seemed to be working miracles, like Christ in the Bible.

Shortly after, another Molokanye made himself canvas wings and tried to fly to heaven from hill tops in the region of Ararat (although only when there was plenty of cloud cover so he could not be seen clearly by onlookers).

IS IT A MIRACLE?

EASTERN PROMISES

China in the nineteenth century was ruled by the Manchus - people who came originally from beyond the northern boundaries of China. The Manchus made all educated non-Manchu men shave the front half of their heads and wear a pigtail.

For this reason (among many others) the Manchus were unpopular with the Chinese. In the middle of the century a young man called Hong Xiuquan led the fight against them. He'd been baptized by a Christian missionary and had decided that he was Jesus's younger brother. Hong started a millenarian movement and called himself king of the 'Heavenly Kingdom of Great Peace' or *Taiping*. By 1850 he had twenty thousand followers.

Hong and his followers rampaged through China. They captured the great city of Nanking and killed all its Manchus, even the children. Wherever they went they destroyed temples and their statues. Hong ordered his followers to sell their property and share everything. All land was to be held in equal amounts and men and women were to be equal.

The Taiping Rebellion lasted from 1850-64. Twenty million people died and six hundred cities were destroyed.

DANCES WITH GHOSTS

In the 1870s, prophets of the Paiute native Americans declared that a new dance, the *Ghost Dance*, must replace the old Native American religious rituals. Then there would be plenty of buffalo again and the spirits of the dead would return. Ghost dances lasted several days. The dancers wore a white garment, the Ghost Shirt, and would dance themselves into a magic trance and exhaustion.

The Ghost Dance spread like wildfire among native Americans. At first, followers were told to live truthfully and be at peace with white settlers, but later, many tribes came to believe that a great earthquake or other such catastrophe would kill the whites and that this 'Millennium' would happen in 1891. This belief was especially strong among the Sioux, where a medicine man called *Chief Sitting Bull* (*c*.1834-1890) claimed that the Dance would protect his people from the bullets of the whites. The government became frightened by the strange behaviour of the dancers, and soldiers were ordered to Sioux lands in case of trouble. In the fighting that followed, Sitting Bull was killed. The last resistance of the Sioux was crushed when over two hundred men, women and children were massacred by white soldiers at *Wounded Knee* in December 1890.

HEAD-HE-GO-ROUND AND BELLY-DON'T-KNOW

By 1900, European power over other people was overwhelming. Fear of white domination led to millenarian ideas in the most remote corners of the world. It was in 1919 that the Australian government first heard about the *Vailala Madness*, so called after the region in Papua New Guinea where it started.

The Vailala Madness was known to the people who suffered from it as 'Head-he-go-round' or 'Belly-don't-know'. Whole villages would collapse into strange stumbling, jabbering behaviour. But it wasn't madness, it was a new millenarian sect: followers believed that the good things of western civilization had been meant for the black people of New Guinea but had been stolen away by the greedy whites before the Papuans could get hold of them. Their prophets foretold that a ship (later sometimes an aeroplane) would arrive bearing the spirits of their ancestors and a cargo of European goods. The ship would herald the start a new age of power and riches.

Leaders of the sect claimed to receive messages from the ancestors either directly from the sky or down specially built village flagpoles. There was no need for anyone to work or farm the land because the ancestors would bring food. Instead, their time was taken up with meaningless military drills and large feasts.

The Vailala Madness continued on and off until 1931. Although no ship came, it was claimed by some that the ground had shaken and a ghostly ship had been seen out at sea. There are still some *Cargo Cults* on remote Pacific Islands to this day.

MEANWHILE BACK IN ENGLAND – THE MILLENNIUM ARRIVES

While all the Ghost Dancing and Head-he-go-rounding had been going on in other parts of the world, English millenarians had kept busy. In 1840, Henry James Prince, a Church of England vicar, announced that he was the returned Messiah to a packed audience in the Assembly Rooms at Weymouth. Prince entered the Rooms to the sound of trumpets. He later started his own sect in the village of Spaxton in Somerset. He kept a pack of bloodhounds and gave titles to his followers such as: 'Angel of the Seventh Seal'.

AND IN AMERICA -

In 1829, William Miller, a New York farmer, prophesied the Second Coming of Christ for 1843 and then changed this to 22 October 1844. He founded the sect of the *Millerites*, or *Second Day Adventists*. Up to 100,000 people in the middle states of America abandoned their homes and businesses as the Great Day approached. They put on gowns of white muslin and took up positions on hilltops and roofs so as to get a good view - but nothing happened.

103

Many Millerites lost faith in Miller's leadership when the Millennium failed to arrive as promised, but some kept heart. They decided that something really had happened in heaven in 1844 although no-one had *seen* it happen. They formed themselves into the *Seventh Day Adventists* in 1863 and are still active today.

JEZREEL'S TOWER

James Rowland White (b.1840) was an English ex-soldier. In 1875, he announced that he was Jezreel, a messenger of God, and that at the 'third watch of the eleventh hour' (i.e. soon) there would be terrible disasters all over the world and the people of all countries would flock to England.

In 1884 the *New and Latter House of Israel*, as White's followers were known, started to build their headquarters on Chatham Hill in Kent. These were to centre round a massive assembly hall housing a revolving electric lantern in the middle of a huge glass dome with a rotating platform underneath it!

The New and Latter House of Israel lived on after Jezreel's death in 1884, but the fantastic building was never finished. Until the 1960s you could still see the start of it, known as *Jezreel's Tower*, on Chatham Hill. Then it was knocked down for redevelopment.

GOTTA GET A WITNESS!

In 1868 a young man called Charles Taze Russell happened to go to a Seventh Day Adventist meeting in America. As a result of what he heard there he took a long hard look at the Bible and decided that Miller had been wrong in his calculations. Russell decided that the Second Coming of Christ would probably happen in 1874. He founded a sect called the *Russellites* or *Millennial Dawnists* to prepare for the Second Coming of Christ. The Russellites were different to mainstream Christians. They believed that God had two sons Christ and the Devil - and that Christ wasn't crucified, he was impaled on a tree.

The Russellites changed their name to *Jehovah's Witnesses* in 1931. They are still active today.

GLOOM, DOOM AND RUIN

Jehovah's Witnesses now believe that Christ probably started his thousand year kingdom in 1914. In which case the First World War (1914-18) must have been the *Battle of Armageddon* prophesied in *Revelation* as the Last Battle (see page 9).

But hold on a moment! What about the Second World War (1939-45)? Or the Korean War? Or the Vietnam War? There have been enough wars in our blood-soaked century to satisfy all the prophets who have ever prophesied. Any of them might have been Armageddon. The problem with prophecies is that you can always find something to fit in with your notion of how things are destined to be.

In fact prophecies and other ideas about the Millennium have affected modern politics ever since the French Revolution - and not always for the best.

In 1797, Francis Dobbs, a member of the Irish House of Commons, claimed that Christ would return either in 1800 or 1801 and free the Irish from British rule. Dobbs died mad and poor in 1811, but at least he was harmless.

Communists believe that there will be a 'Revolution' after which all people will live together as equals, sharing their property. So communists are millenarians in the sense that they believe that a time will come when the world will be almost perfect. The communist revolution which started in Russia in 1917 resulted in the deaths of more than twenty million people.

On 5 September 1934, shortly before the start of the Second World War, Adolf Hitler announced to a mass rally of thousands of his Nazi supporters that Germans would rule the world for a thousand years, the *Thousand Year Reich*. Hitler and his Nazis failed to establish their evil empire - though not for want of trying.

Let's be grateful that most of these modern prophecies are no more reliable than Armageddon and the return of the Beast. There's been more than enough gloom, doom and millenarian madness in the world over the last 2,000 years.

How the world will actually end

Scientists now think that the world will end about six billion years from now (that's *six million* millenniums). At that time the Sun will expand into a *red giant* and Earth will be burnt to a frazzle.

THE SURFACE OF EARTH WILL BE A DRIED-OUT DESERT.

ANY SURVIVORS WILL HAVE TO LIVE UNDERGROUND, PROTECTED FROM THE SUN'S HEAT.

HUMANS WILL LONG SINCE HAVE BEEN REPLACED BY OTHER CREATURES.

TELL ME ABOUT THE BEAST, DAD!

109

THINGS TO DO AT THE END OF THE WORLD

Perhaps the prophets of doom are right and the End will come sooner than the scientists expect. The twentieth century has been long and bloody. There's not much you can do to save yourself if the Beast appears at the end of it:

Hide under the bedclothes and pretend it isn't happening.

Die and go to heaven.

Try to make friends with the Beast.

WOULD YOU LIKE A CHOCO-POP?

Die and go to hell.

TIME FOR A CELEBRATION

POOH TO PROPHECIES!

It's time to forget all the crazy prophets and their crazy prophecies. It's time to celebrate that the world's still here, that there's been no Millennium, no Second Coming, no storms, earthquakes and other disasters at least not big enough to End the World. It's time to celebrate that with luck there could be another thousand years of life and history ahead of us, that the millennium is just a date plucked out of the air - and a jolly good excuse for a party!

TIME FOR A CHANGE

But stop! Have you worked out when *exactly* you should start covering yourself in honey, popping two thousand balloons, bathing in lemonade or whatever else you have in mind? Why should it be midnight at the end of 1999 as everyone assumes it will be? Why not quarter to midnight? Or half past eight? Or ten to six the previous evening?

It all depends when you think the millennium begins. Days haven't always begun at midnight:

Until 1925, astronomers counted the days from midday to midday.

 Astronomers are people who study the stars and planets.

Most primitive peoples think
the day starts with the dawn.

The Ancient Jews and
Greeks counted the days
from sunset to
sunset.

The Ancient Germans counted nights.
That's where we get the word
'fortnight', meaning 'fourteen nights'.

WHY JANUARY 1ST?

And another thing - the millennium doesn't have
to start on 1 January: the Ancient Egyptian New
Year was in July when Sirius the Dog Star first
appeared over the horizon. In Britain and much of
Europe, New Year's Day was once 26 December,
the day after Christmas. In the fourteenth century
it was 25 March - the complications never cease!

TIME LINES

Of course it all depends where you are. Clocks tell
different times at the same real time in different parts
of the world, travelling from east to west or west to

east. So when it's 23.59 pm in central Australia it's only 14.59 pm in Britain (depending on whether England is on summer or winter time, when the clocks change by an hour).

This is because the Earth is round: the Sun can only shine on half of it at any one moment, and where there's sunlight we call it daylight and where there's shadow we call it night. If all clocks told the same time, then someone somewhere would have to have their morning at midnight just so someone else could have it at the proper time!

The clocks in your school don't tell a different time to the clocks in your home any more than your clock tells a different time to the other clocks in your country (or a section of your country if you live somewhere big like Australia or Canada). In other words, the time that clocks show doesn't change gradually as we slip from east to west or vice versa. It changes in sudden jumps. One moment it's five o'clock; one step to the east into a different *time zone* and it's six o'clock. That's why people in different parts of the world will be celebrating the millennium at different starting times.

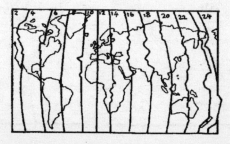

Some standard time zones. Numbers at the top show times with London at 12 o'clock

DATELINE

Time zones are roughly divided by lines of longitude. Look at the lines of longitude on a map of the world and you will see that the line that runs through London (or Greenwich to be precise) is labelled zero. In fact all time in the world is counted plus or minus from the time at Greenwich in London, which is known as *Greenwich Mean Time*. The *Universal Day* begins at midnight in Greenwich.

GREENWICH

LINES OF LONGITUDE

However Greenwich is not where most people think the new millennium will begin, because Greenwich is on the other side of the world to the *International Date Line*. This is a zig zag line drawn down the middle of the Pacific Ocean as far away from people as possible. It's the magic line where one day turns into another, where if you're travelling east you go back to yesterday, and if you're travelling west you go forward to tomorrow! The International Date Line is just to the east of Chatham Island, where this book started.

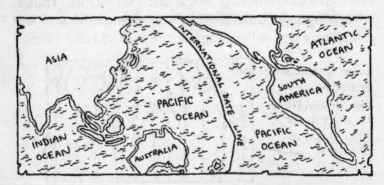

This seems a little unfair on Greenwich. Surely the Zero Meridian should be the same as the International Date Line?

No chance. Sorry Londoners but Greenwich is out. Just think for a minute: if the Zero Meridian and the International Date Line were the same thing, then Kent and East Anglia which are to the east of London would have to be in a different day to the rest of England, otherwise each new day could not start at Greenwich. If we want the millennium to start at Greenwich then we have to accept that when it's Wednesday in England it will only be Tuesday in Kent!

That's why the millennium will start near Chatham Island. The International Date Line really does need to be as far away from people as possible!

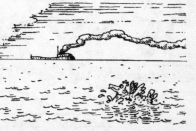

AT LAST – LET THE CELEBRATIONS BEGIN!

All right, no more quibbling. It's 11.59 pm (or 23.59 on a 24 hour clock), 31 December 1999 wherever you are in the world. The millennium is almost upon us. It's time to think seriously about a celebration:

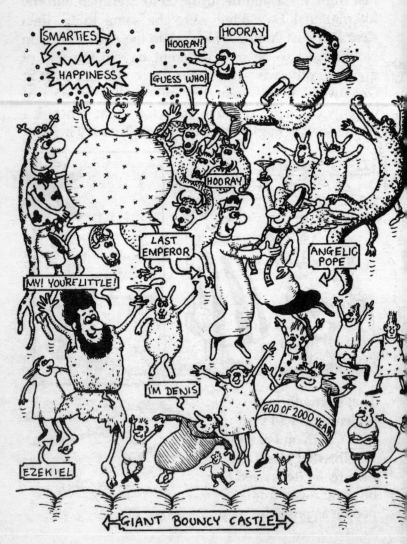

ONE LAST SUGGESTION

The Ancient Aztecs could tell us a thing or two about how to celebrate the millennium (see page 8):

In the Aztec system a new era dawned every fifty-two years, and after every fifty-two years they believed that the world was in danger of coming to an end, so in a sense they had a Millennium every fifty-two years. The fifty-second year always ended on a day known as *Year 1 Rabbit*.

On the night of *Year 1 Rabbit* people feared that the Sun would fail to rise in the morning. All fires were put out, cups and plates were broken and statues of the gods thrown into water. Women and small children had to stay indoors because it was feared that the women would turn into wild animals and the children into mice. Then priests dressed as gods kindled a fire on the breast of a human victim. As the flames flickered they ripped the heart from his chest and soon threw it into the newly-kindled fire.

Fires were then lit from the new fire. The Aztecs could relax: they knew that the Sun would appear in the morning. (Actually they believed it would be an entirely new Sun.) The world had been saved from destruction.

If we want to make really sure that the new millennium arrives safely, we could perform this ceremony at Stonehenge!

IT'S ALL OVER

Enough of victims! Enough of celebrations! This book has taken you through two thousand years of madness, maths and misunderstandings. Imagine, now you're in the year 2000. What are your hopes and prophecies for the future? There's one at least you will probably agree with:

For the time being at any rate!

ANSWERS TO SUPER QUIZ

Page 7   *Score 5 points each for mildew and Aunt Mildred.* All the rest are based on *mille*, including 'mile' - a Roman mile was a thousand paces, hence the name of it.

Page 16   You would be a year older than you are now. *This is a very simple question: score zero for the correct answer and minus 5 for an incorrect answer because you must have a tadpole-sized brain!*

Page 21   Greyhound number 7 wins the race. (7×7=49, 49+160=209, 209+30=239, 239×10=2,390, 2,390-290=2,100, 2,100-100=2,000!). *Score ten if you chose the winning dog, nothing if you chose the wrong dog, and minus five if you chose the wrong dog first time and then tried again - that's cheating!*

Page 23   3,000 is written MMM in Roman. *Score no points for a correct answer and minus five for an incorrect one - you need to get your brain cleaned out!*

THERE WE ARE- CLEAN AS A WHISTLE! WE'LL JUST POP IT BACK IN.

1 c. Chiliasm is belief in the return of Christ to rule for a thousand years. It's based on the Greek *khilioi* meaning a thousand, which *kilogram* and *kilometre* also come from, although 'chiliasm' is spelled differently. *Score five points for the correct answer, none for b. and minus 2 for a.*

2 b. See page 43 - some prophets wore camel-hair cloaks with leather belts. *Score 5 for the correct answer, none for c. and minus 2 for a.*

3 a. See page 45 - Nero was so unpopular at the time of the fire that he needed someone else to blame for it. Christians were the ideal scapegoats. *Score 5 for the correct answer, and minus 2 for b. & c.*

4 a. See page 41 - the Book of Genesis in the Bible says that God made the world in six days and on the seventh he rested. *Score 5 for the correct answer and minus 2 for b. & c.*

5 b. This quiz is to find out if you would have passed as an early Christian, and they believed that Christ would return within their lifetimes. *Score 5 for the correct answer.*

6 a. 'Phurtlis' was a word spoken by Russian millenarians in the fourteenth century (see page 50). It would have meant nothing to an early Christian. *Score 5 for the correct answer.*

7 b. See page 43 - Greek seers spoke with frenzied lips. *Score 5 for the correct answer.*

8 b. See page 49 - Christians who died for their faith as martyrs went to heaven automatically. *Score 5 for the correct answer.*

Page 69

1 b. See page 66/67 - Protestants don't like the idea of a Pope as leader of the church; they prefer to make up their own minds about their faith. *Score 5 for the correct answer.*

2 c. See page 62 - there was no 'Germany' in those days, only the Holy Roman Empire which included parts of Italy and Eastern Europe. *Score 5 for the correct answer.*

3 b. See page 48 - Gog and Magog were barbarian tribes. *Score 5 for the correct answer.*

4 c. and possibly a bit of b. see page 61, after all the Angelic Pope isn't real. *Score 5 for c. and 3 for b.*

5 a. See page 64. *Score 5 for the correct answer.*

Page 84 The questions on page 84 are to find out if you are mad but you score *minus* points for the crazy answers - because it's not a good thing to be mad!

1 a. or b. See page 80. *Score minus 10 for a. because only a really mad person would separate the sticks and stones and then stack them neatly. Score minus 5 for b. because you've got to be mad to do it at all!*

2 a. or b. See page 81 for Lady Eleanor Davis. *Score minus 10 for b. because it's mad and nasty and minus 5 for a. because it's mad but only stupid.*

3 a. or c. See page 80. *Score minus 10 for a. but only minus 5 for c. because c. is a reasonable question to ask - if you're a mad person.*

1 b. See page 90. *Score 10 for the correct answer and 5 for a. because this page is designed to find out if you're a believer, and you're definitely a believer if you think Mary could have given birth to any rabbits at all!*

2 c. See page 93. *Score 10 for the correct answer and 2 for b., because you're still a believer if you think Joanna Southcott gave birth at 64.*

3 a. See page 88. *Score 10 for the correct answer and 5 for c. because you're still a believer if you think Emes will come back from the dead some time.*

FINAL SCORES

115. Maximum possible score, you have won the super quiz. You may well be a super-being with super-powers who will be seen by the entire universe at the Millennium (see page 95).

Above 70. Not bad - you're no super-being, but you'll do.

Below 50. Mediocre, read this book again - and this time, learn it!

Below 10. Bad, learn to read, then read this book again.

Below minus 20. Absolutely awful. Go find a Taborite and ask him to do you in.

INDEX

About the Author

Bob Fowke is a well-known author of children's information books. Writing under various pen names and with various friends and colleagues, he has created around fifty unusual and entertaining works on all manner of subjects.

There's always more to his books than meets the eye (just check out the index at the back of this one!). They're just the thing if you want your brain to bulge and your information banks to burble.

He spent his own childhood in the large, draughty vicarage of the village of Fletching in Sussex (where the famous historian Edward Gibbon is buried). A Church of England vicarage may seem far removed from some of the wilder sects described in this book - but maybe on dark nights it gave the young Fowke a few ideas about the Millennium!

Have you tried any of the books in this series, also published by Hodder Children's Books?

WHAT THEY DON'T TELL YOU ABOUT ...